Mandala Coloring Book for Kids
Activity Book Inspire Creativity

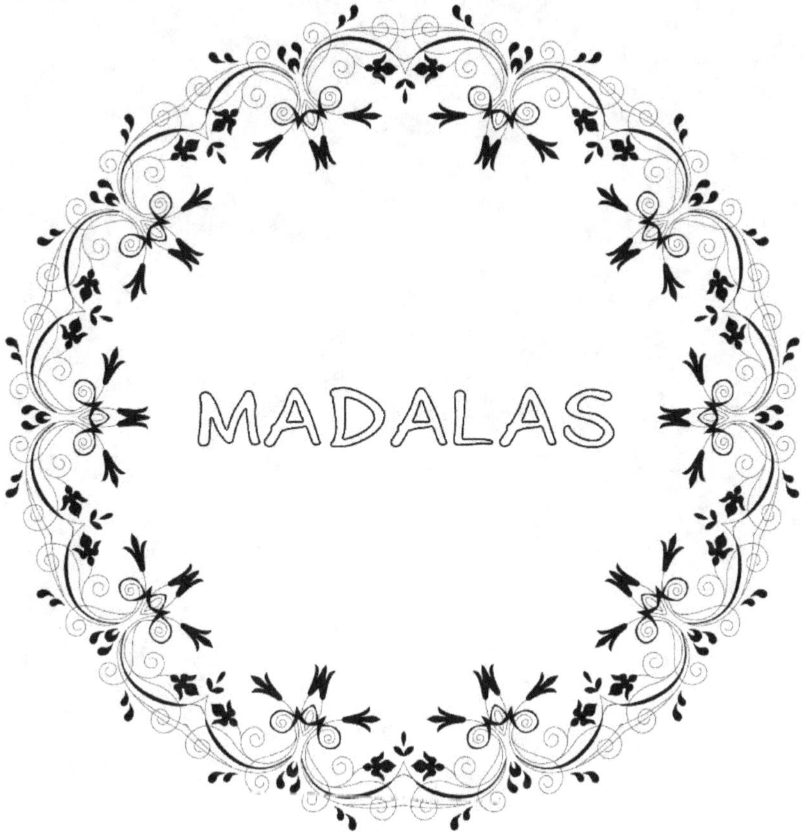

Annie Jr.

Mandala Coloring Book for Kids
Activity Book Inspire Creativity

Copyright: Published in the United States by Annie Jr.
Published January 2017

ISBN-13: 978-1542648837

ISBN-10: 1542648831

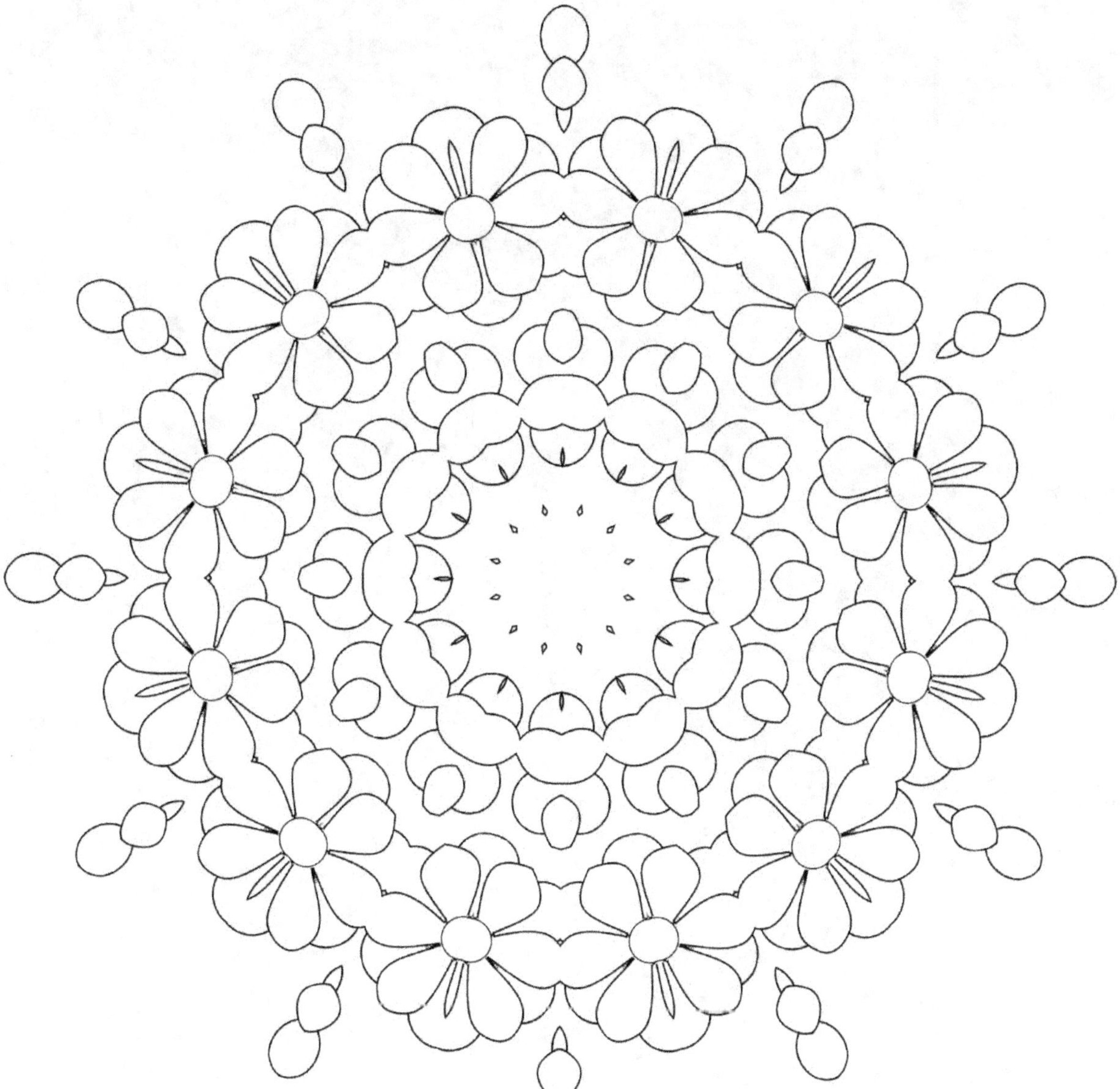

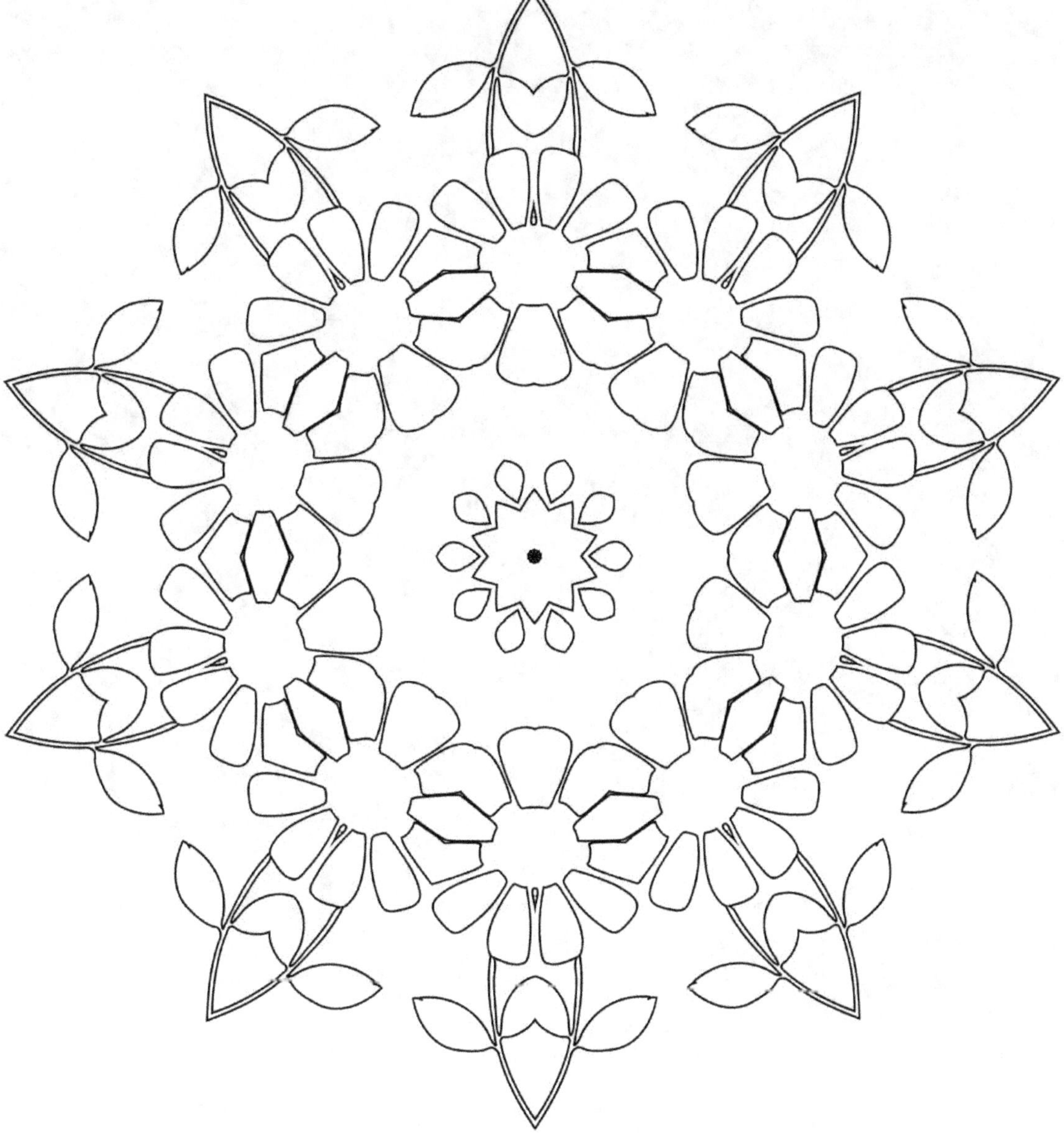

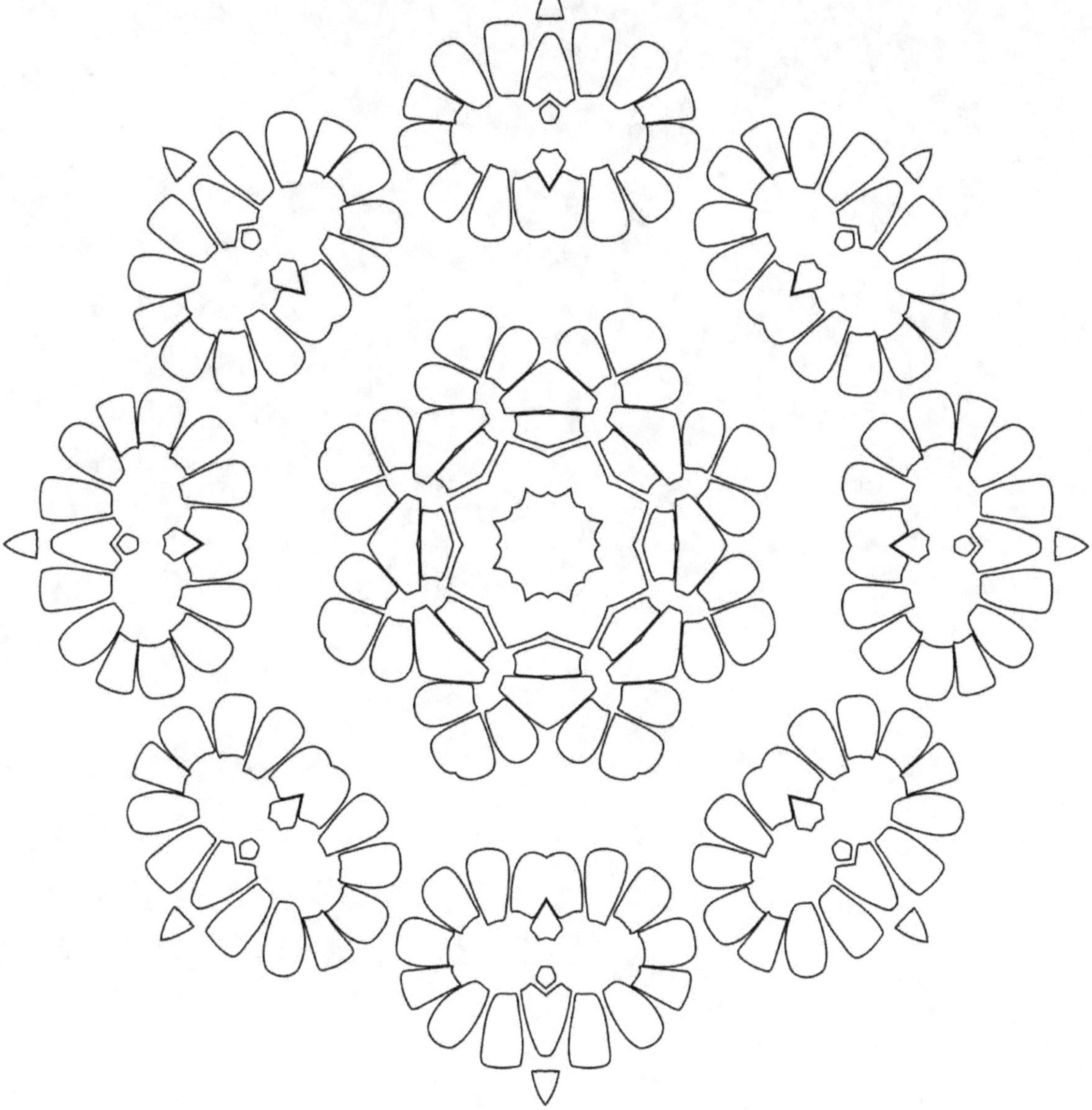

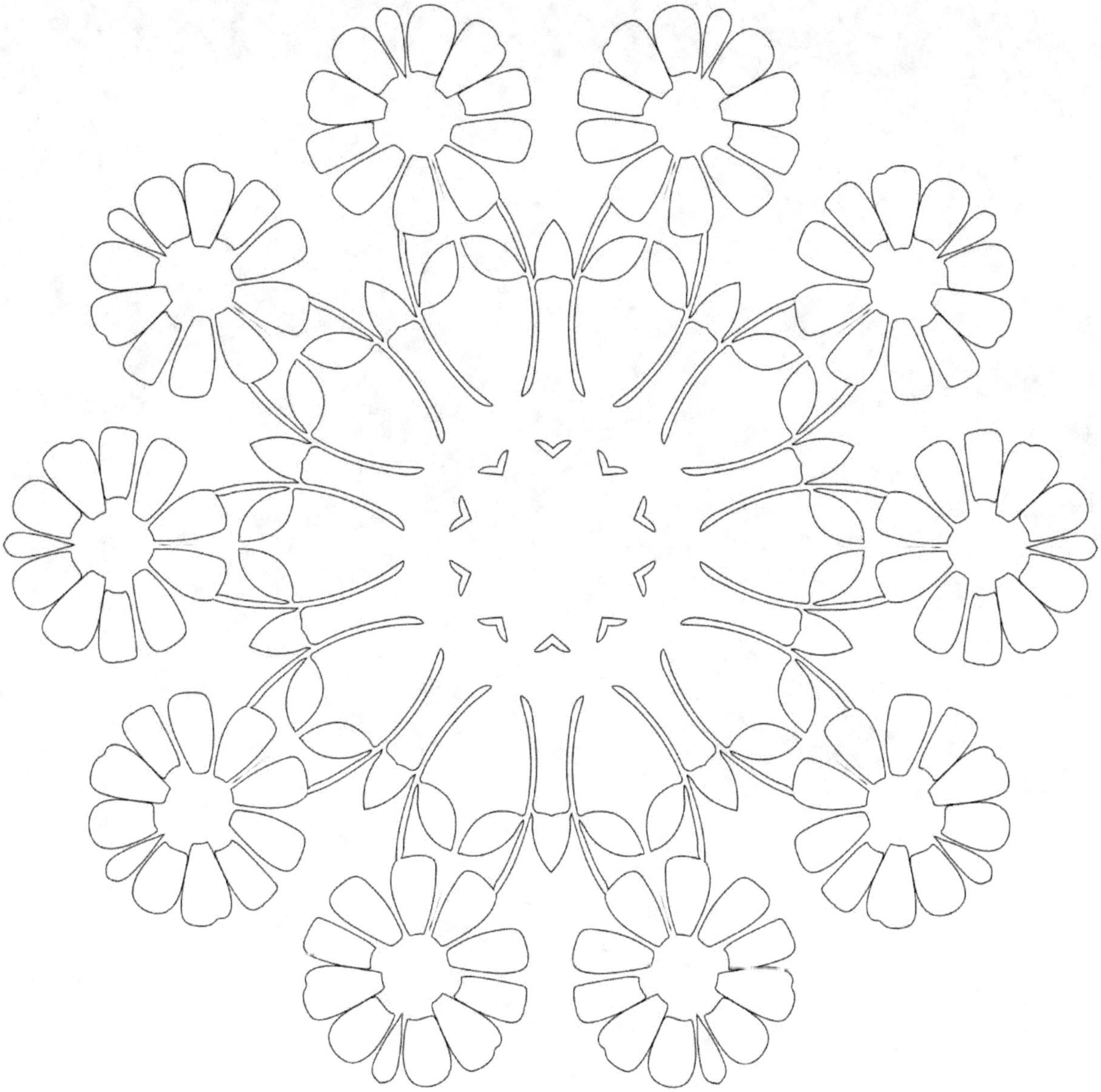

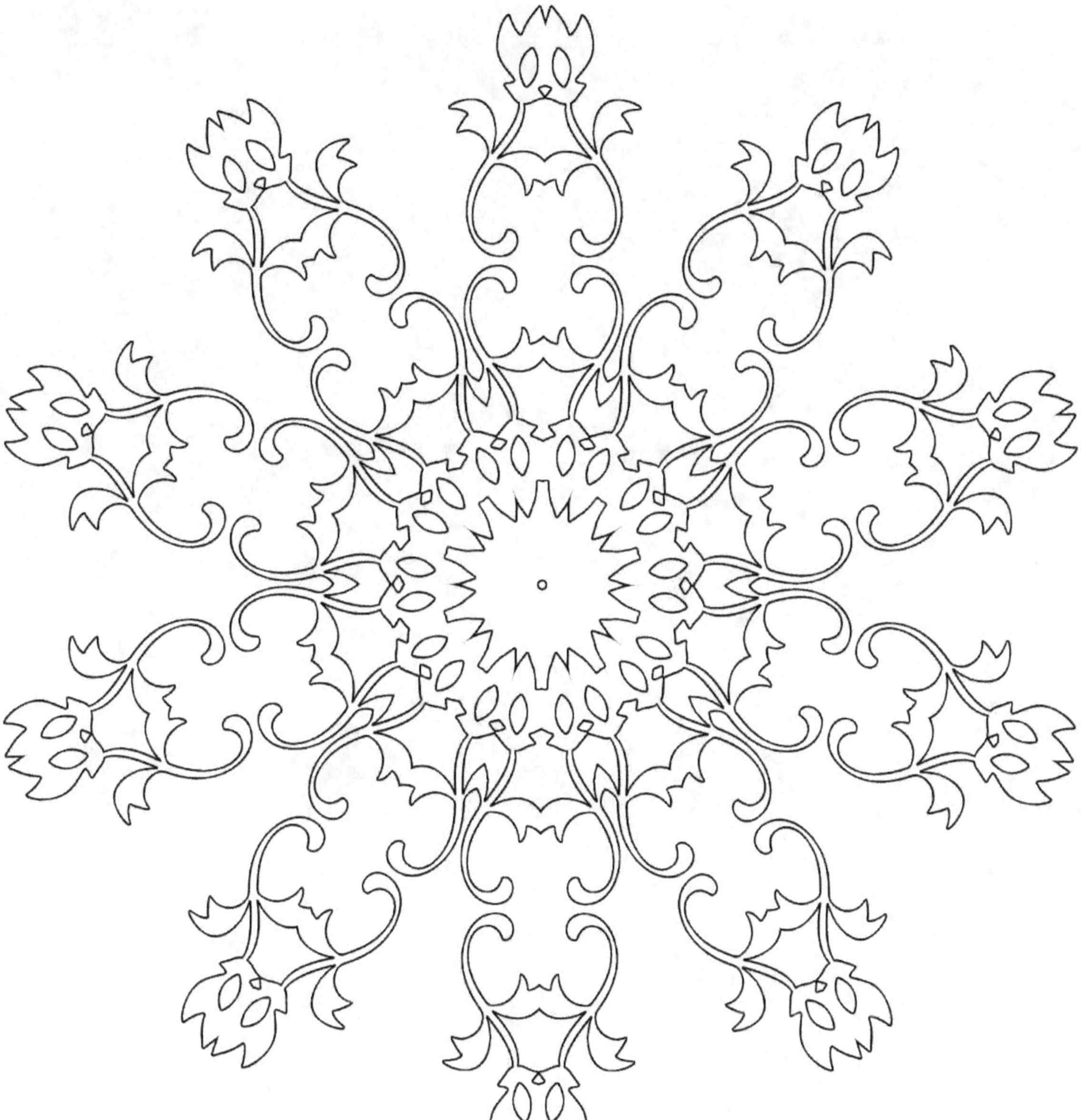

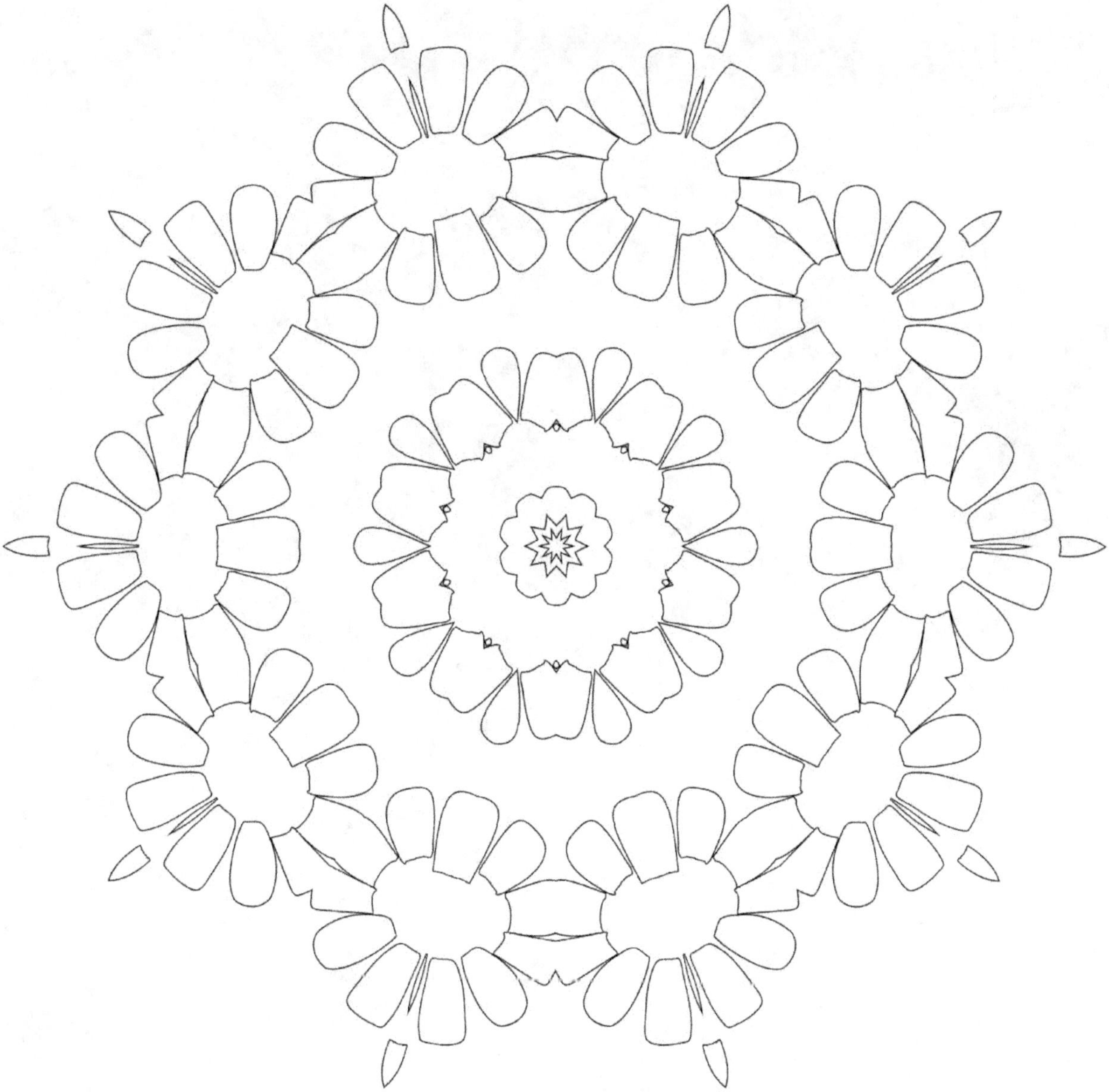

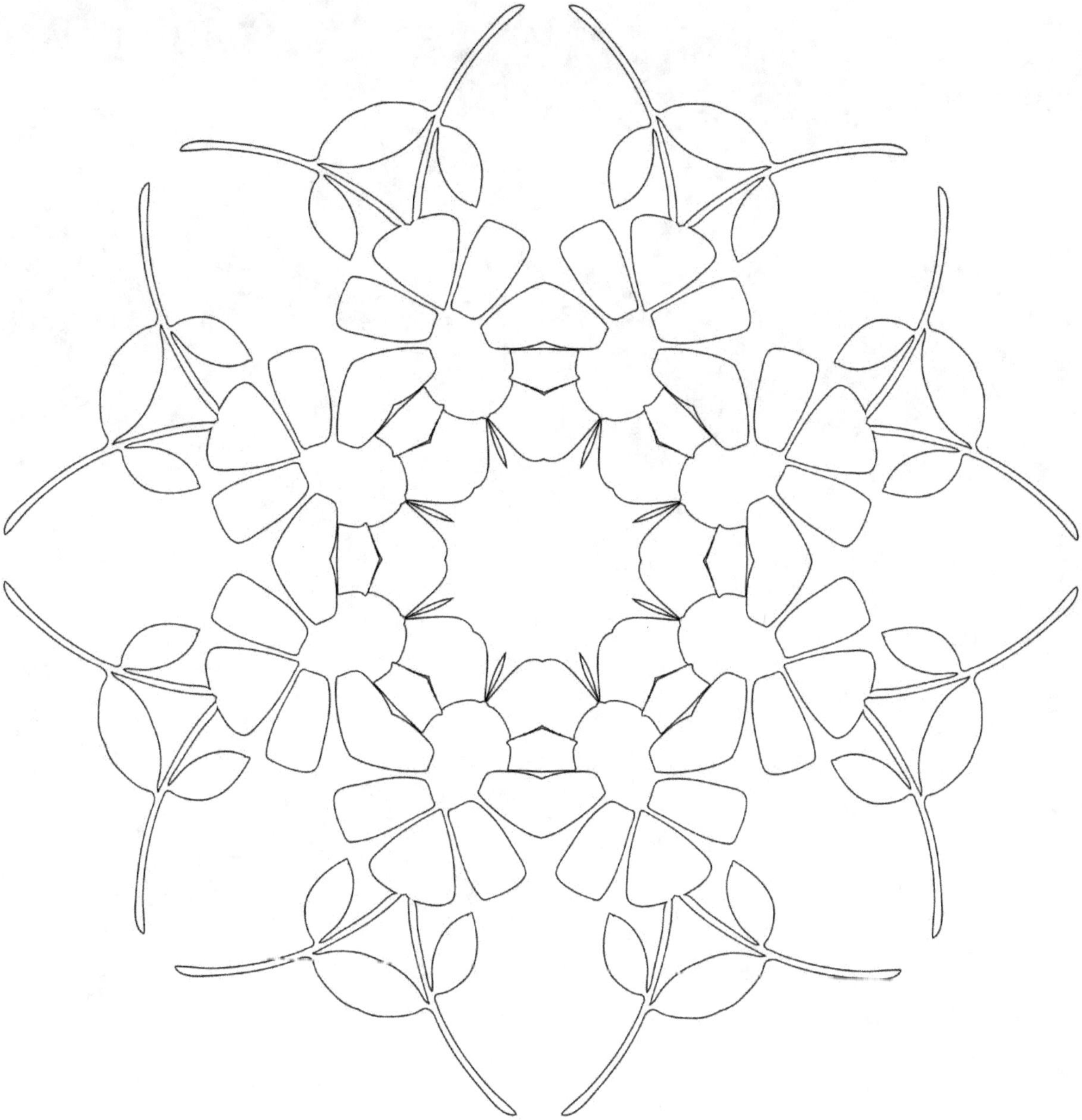

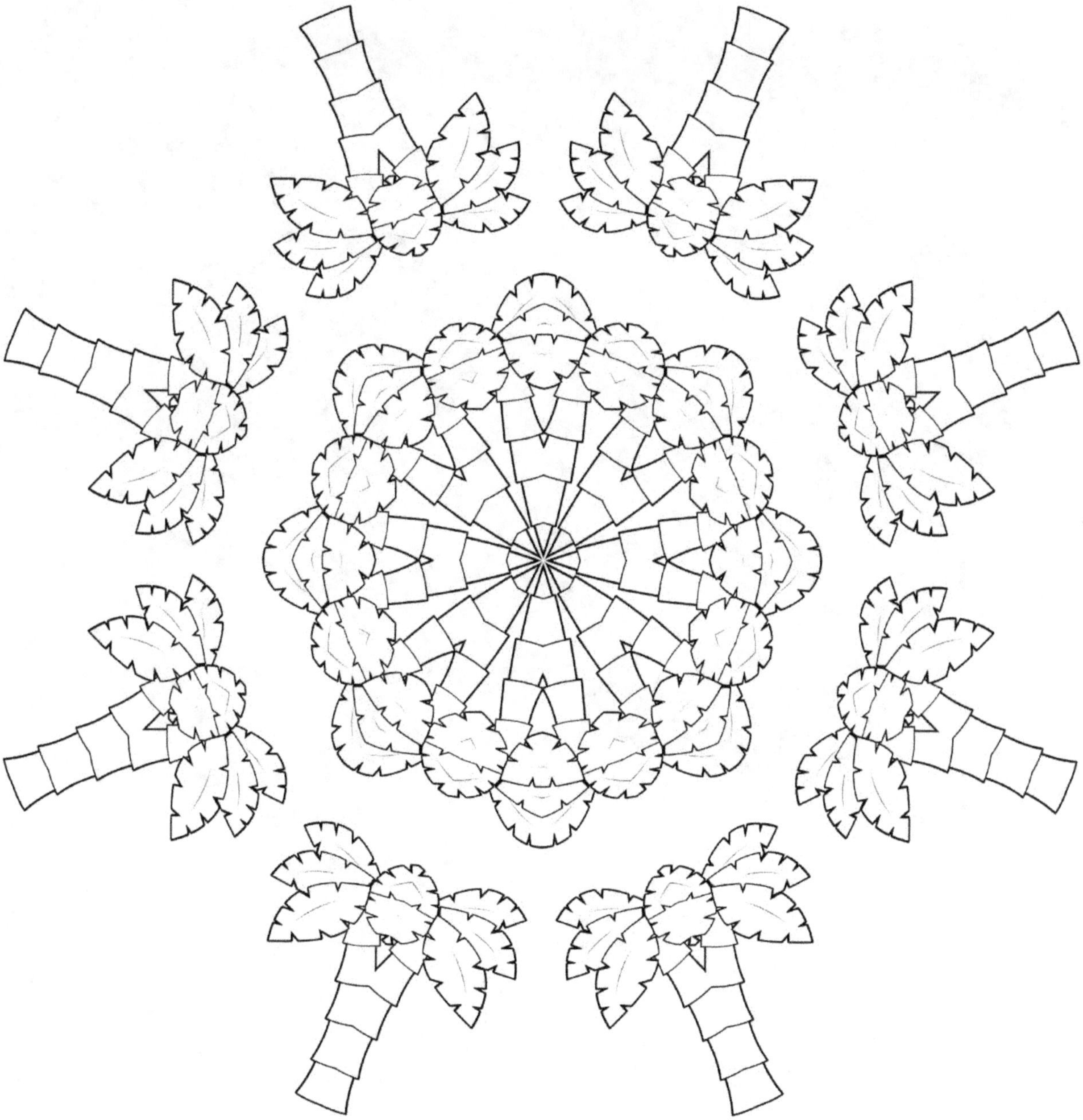

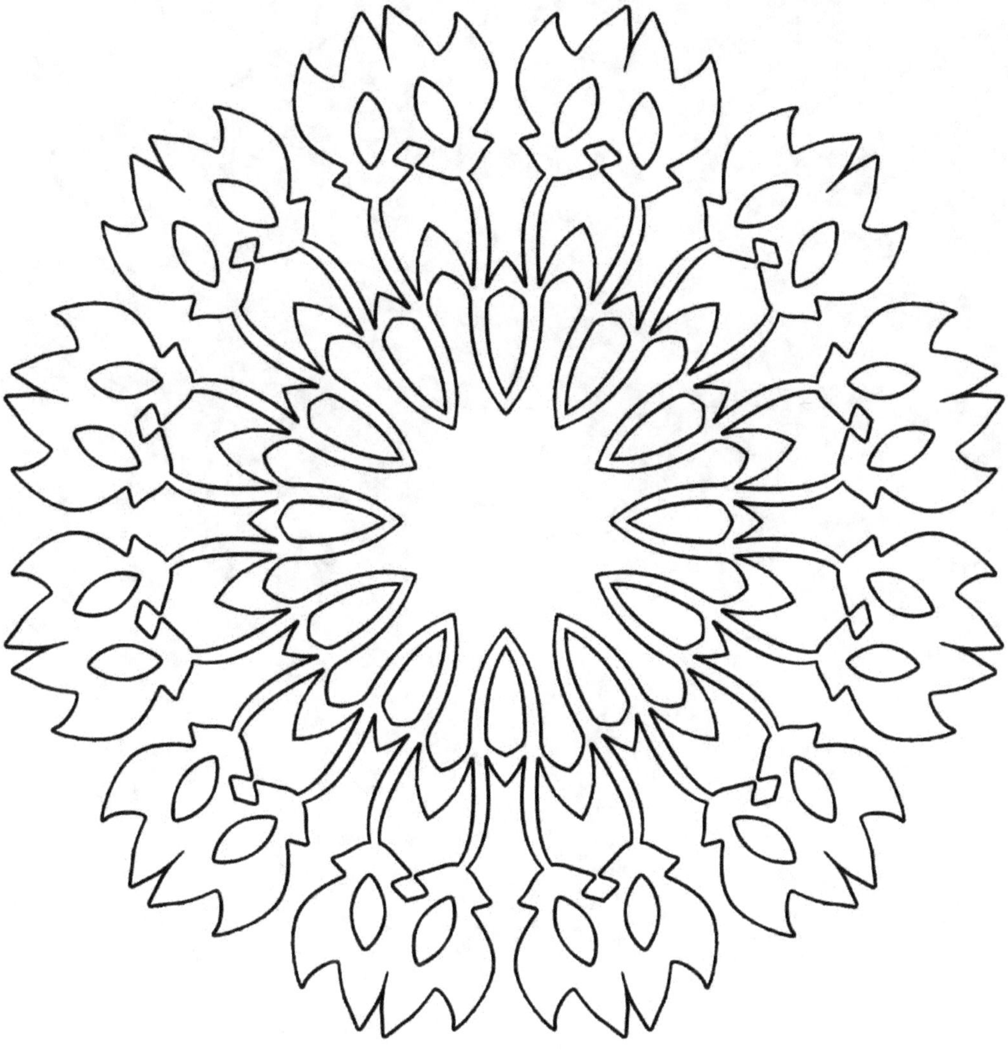

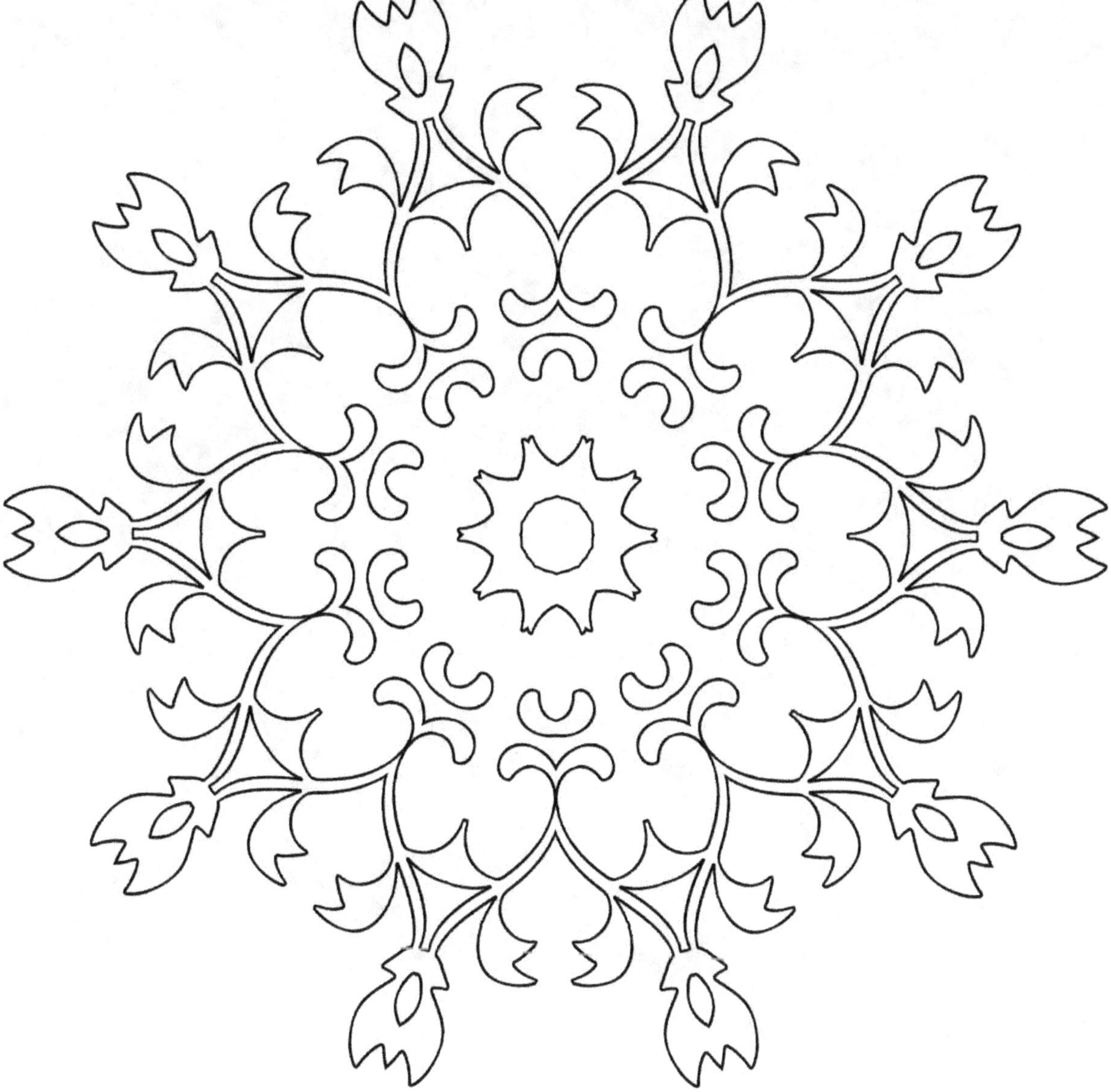

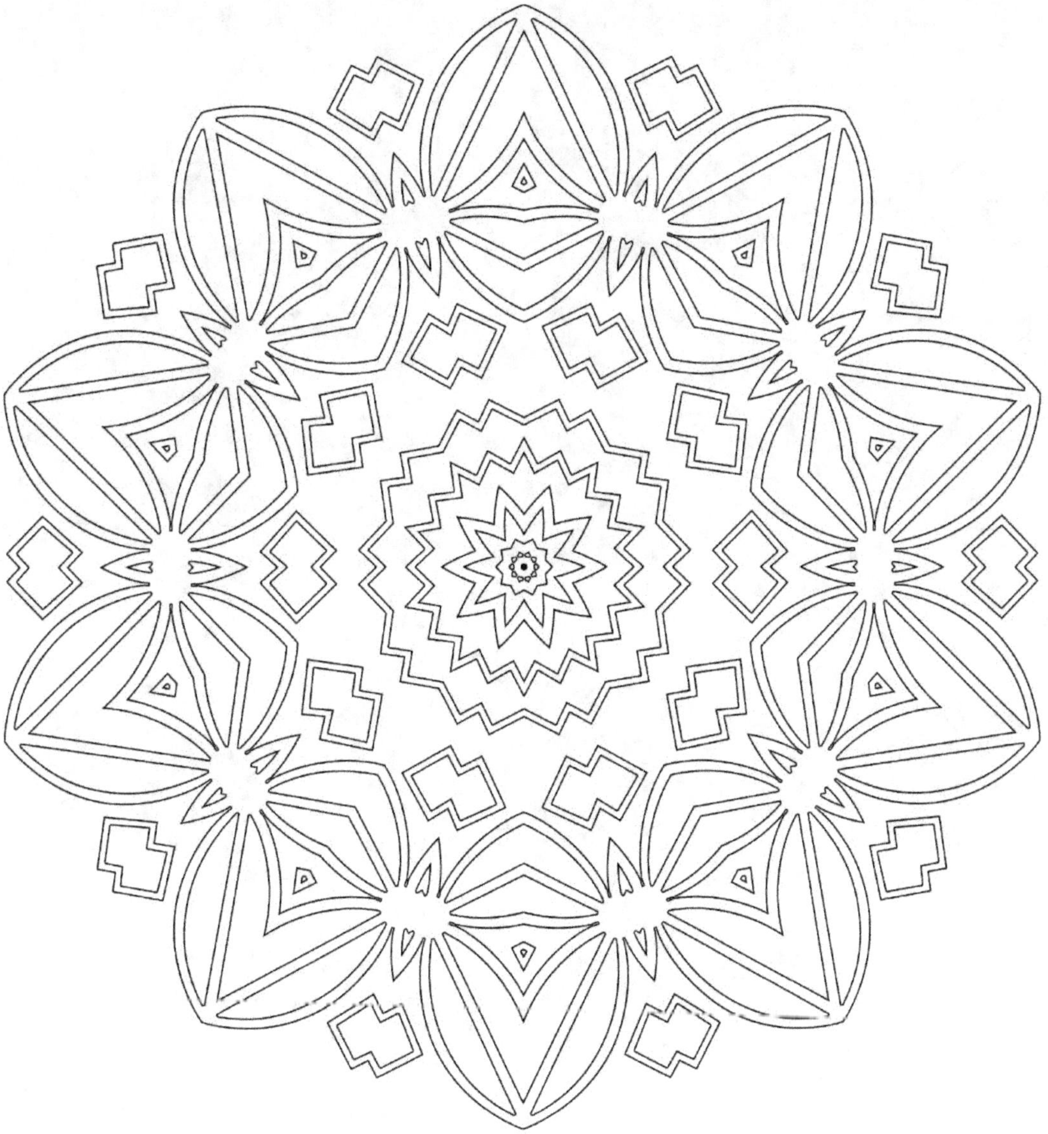

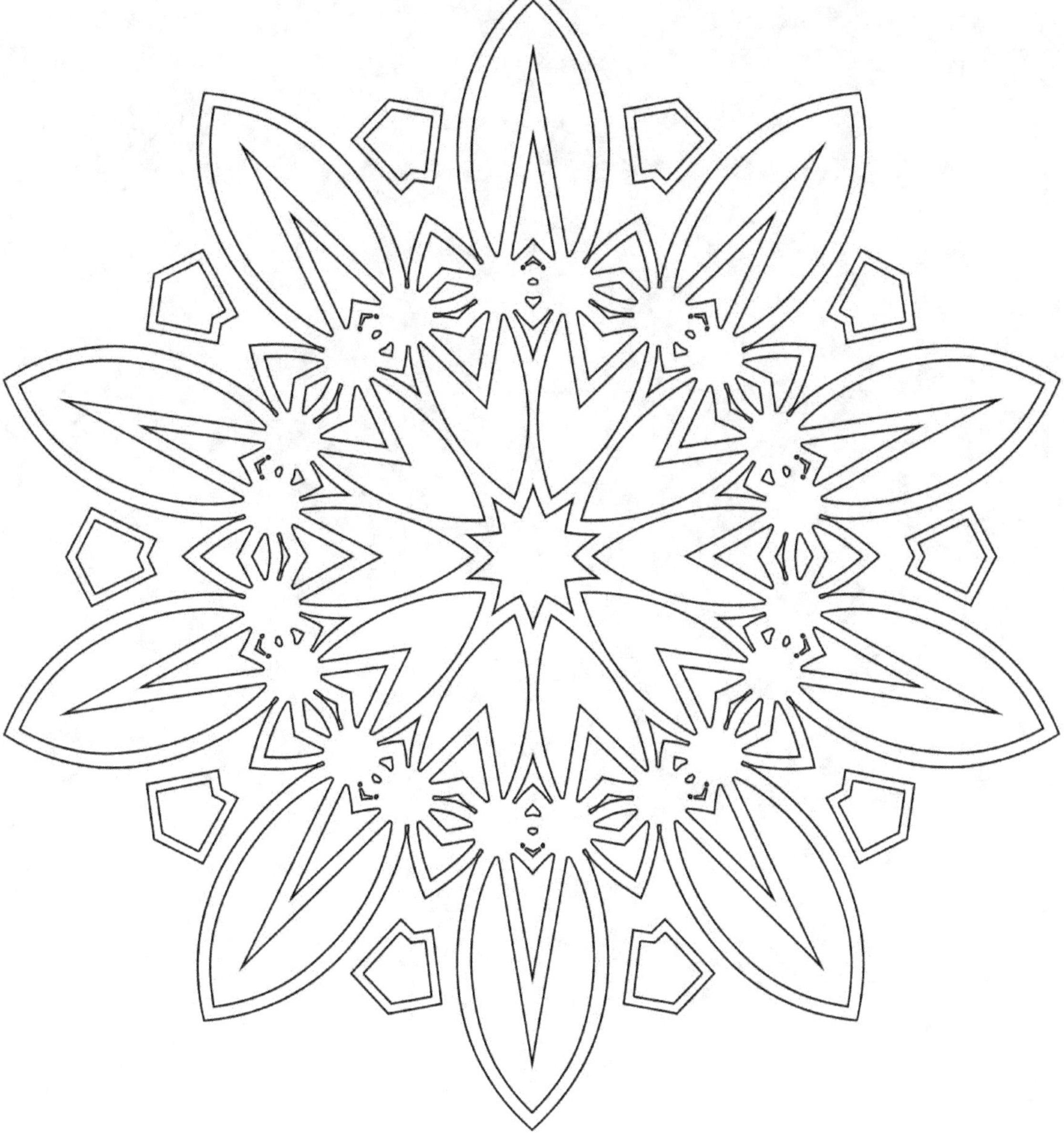

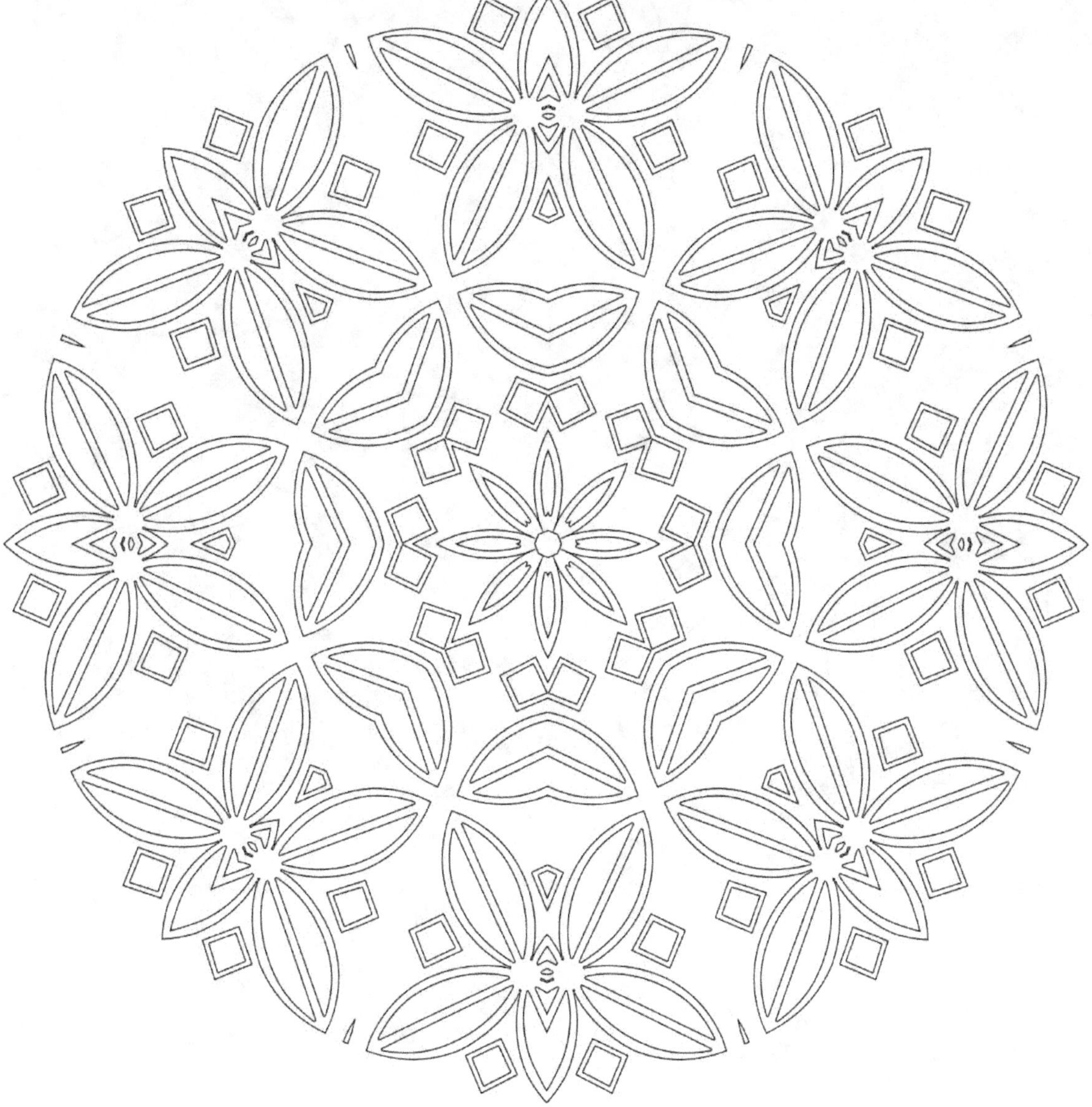

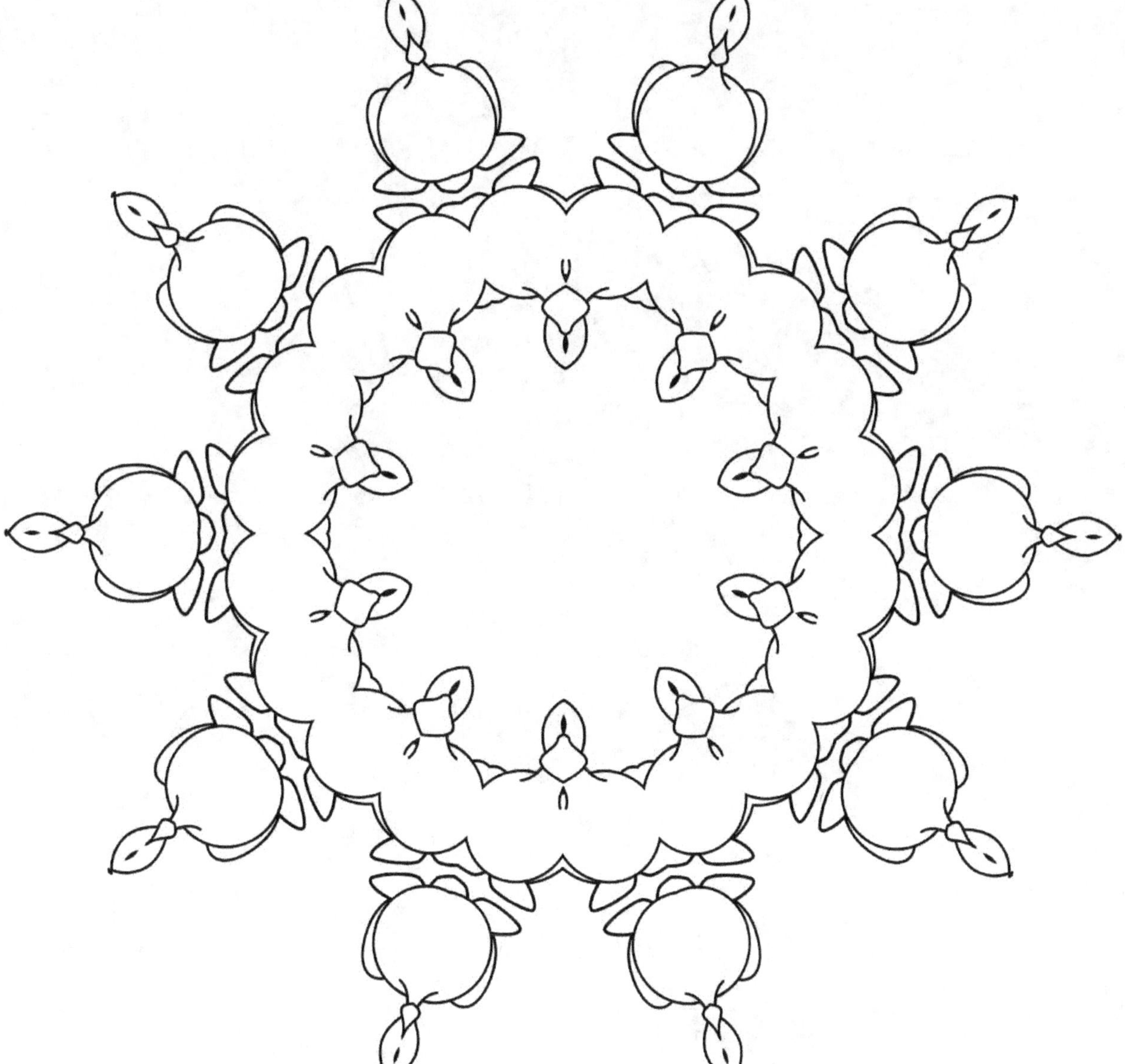

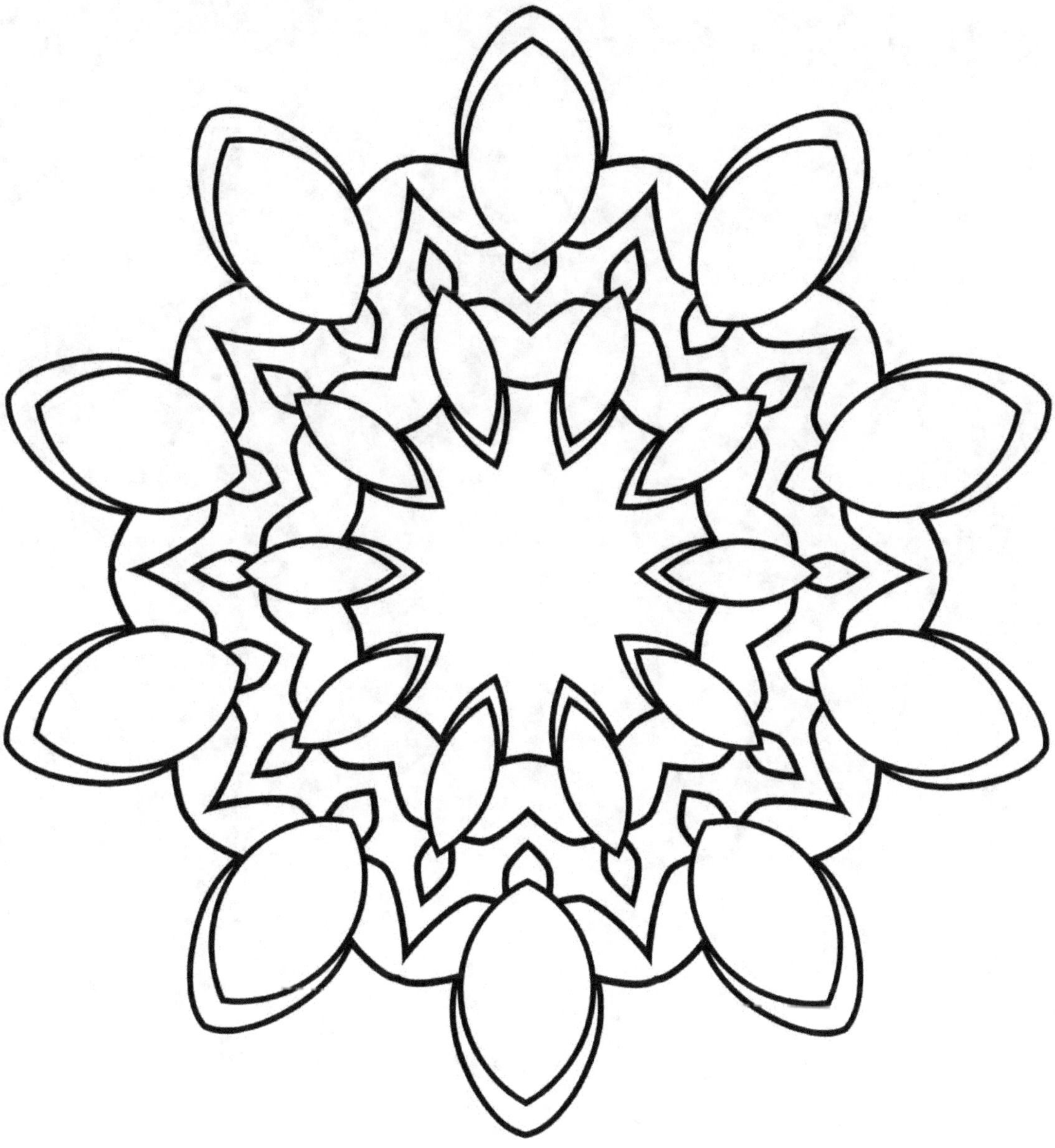

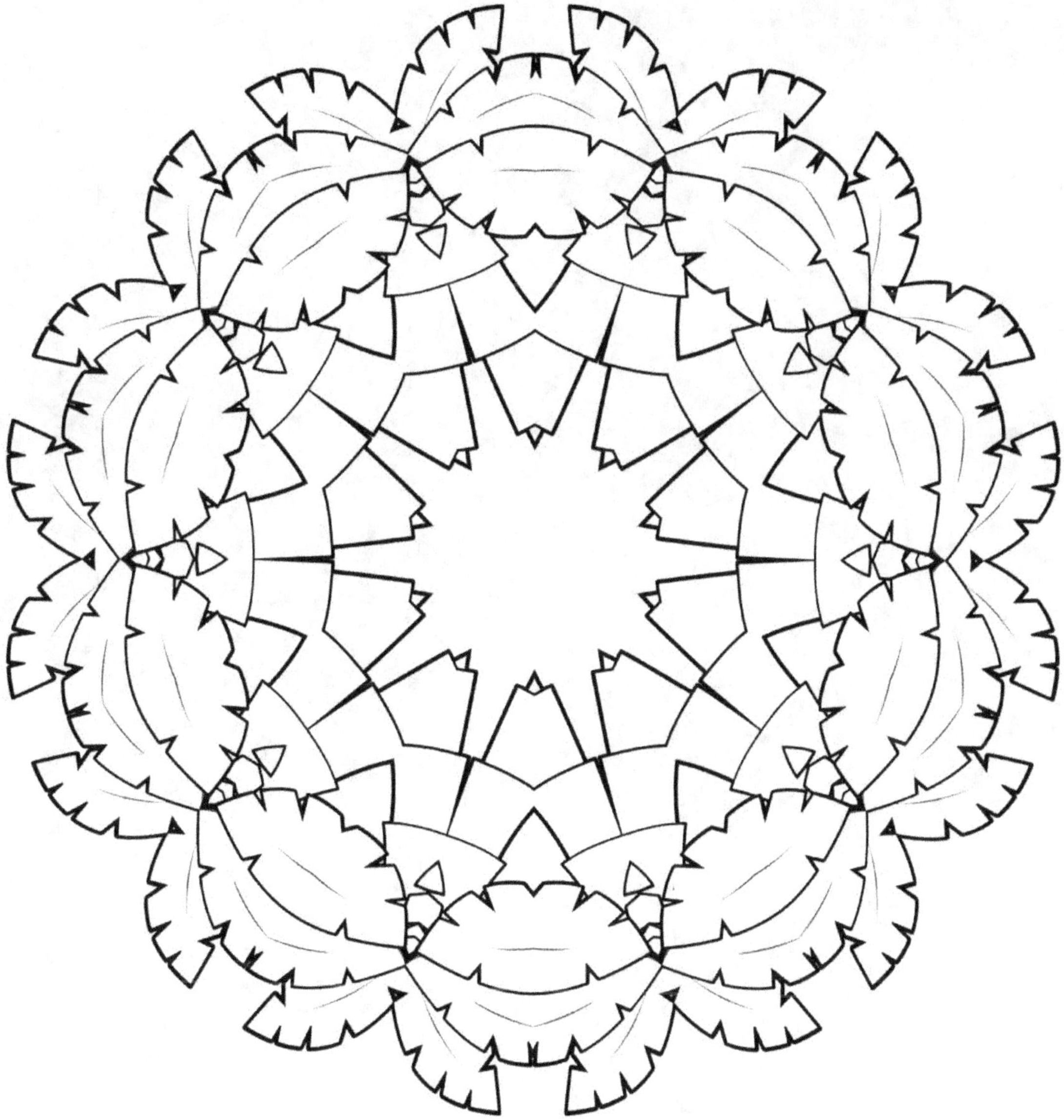

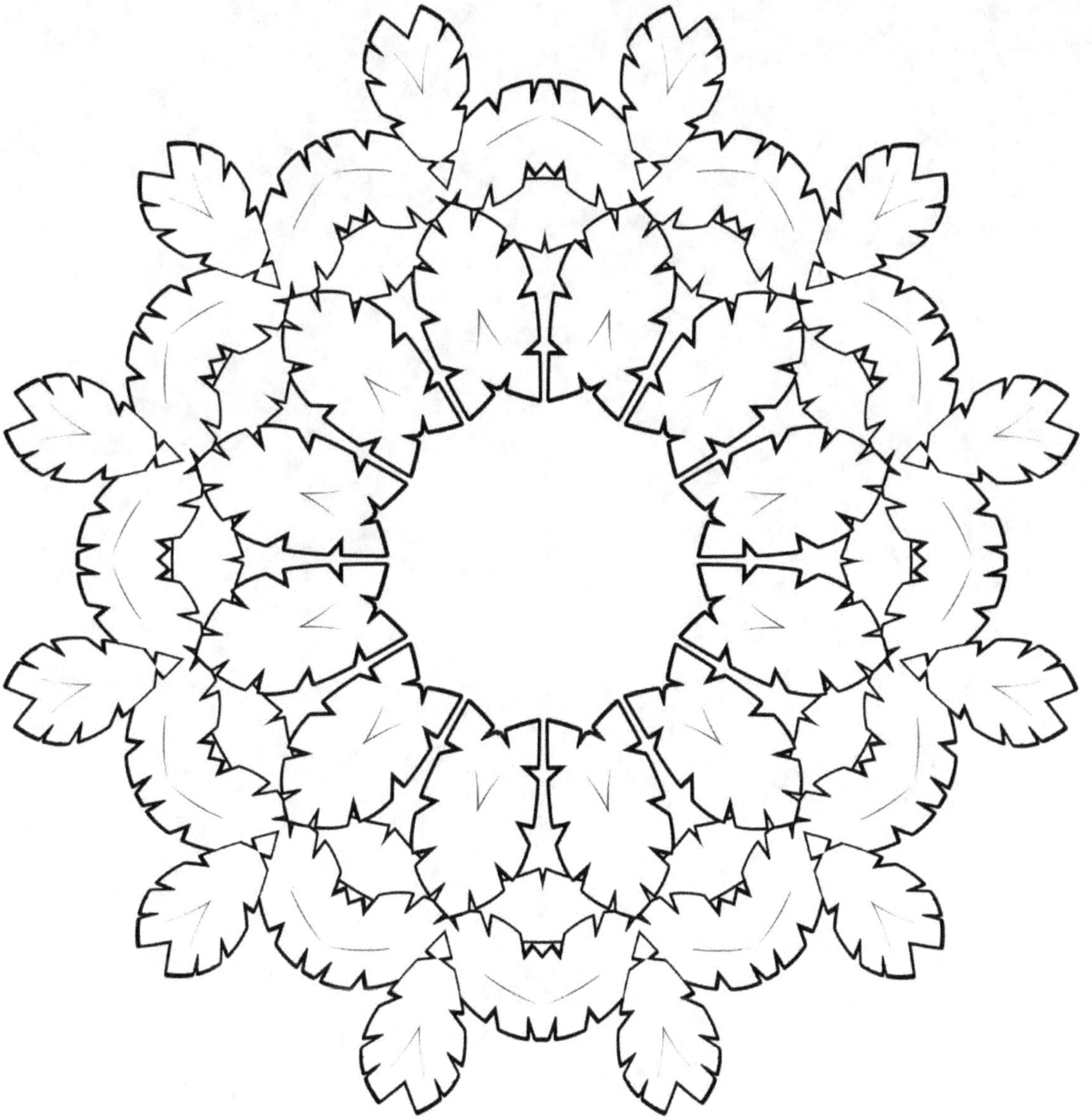

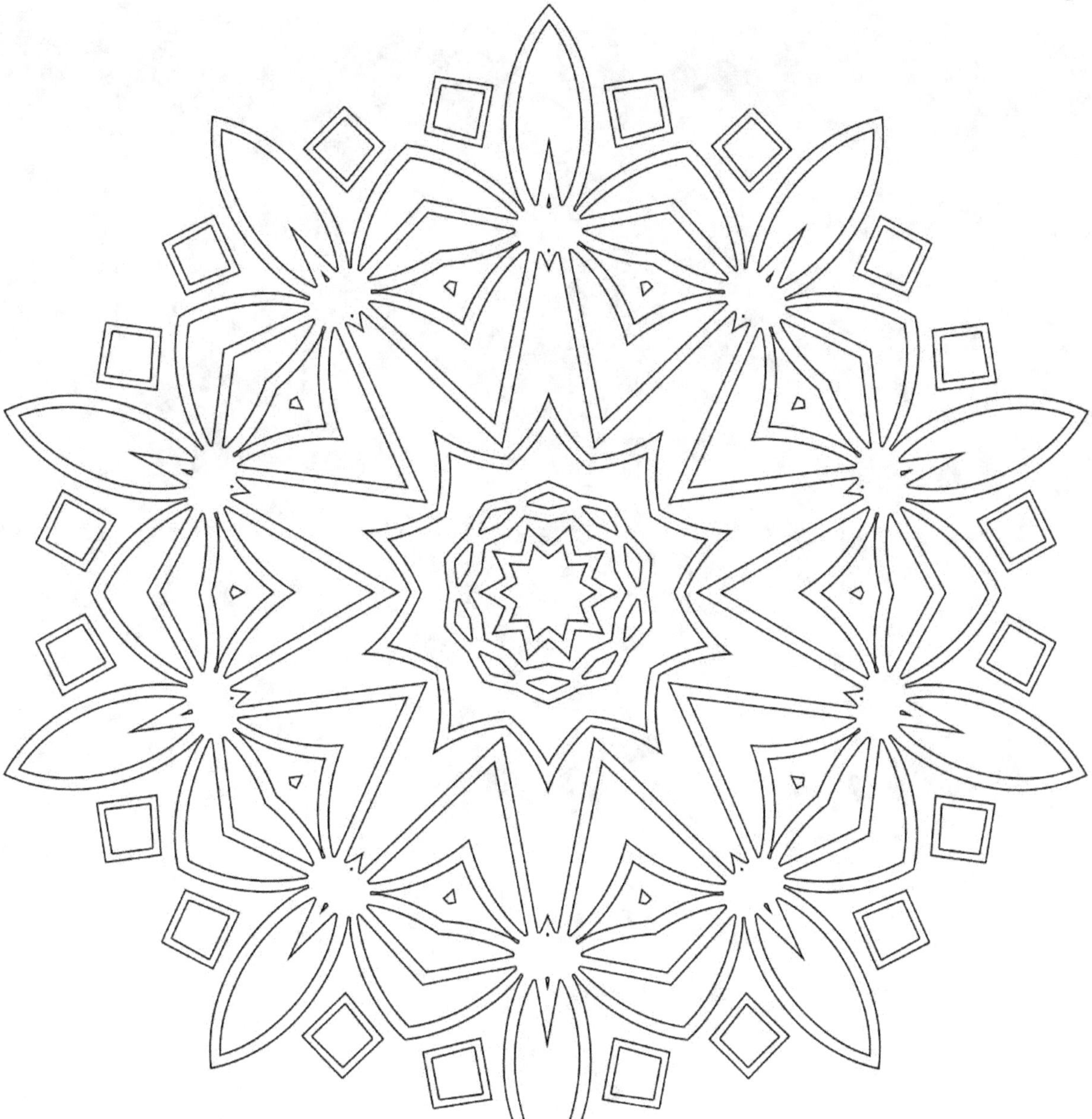

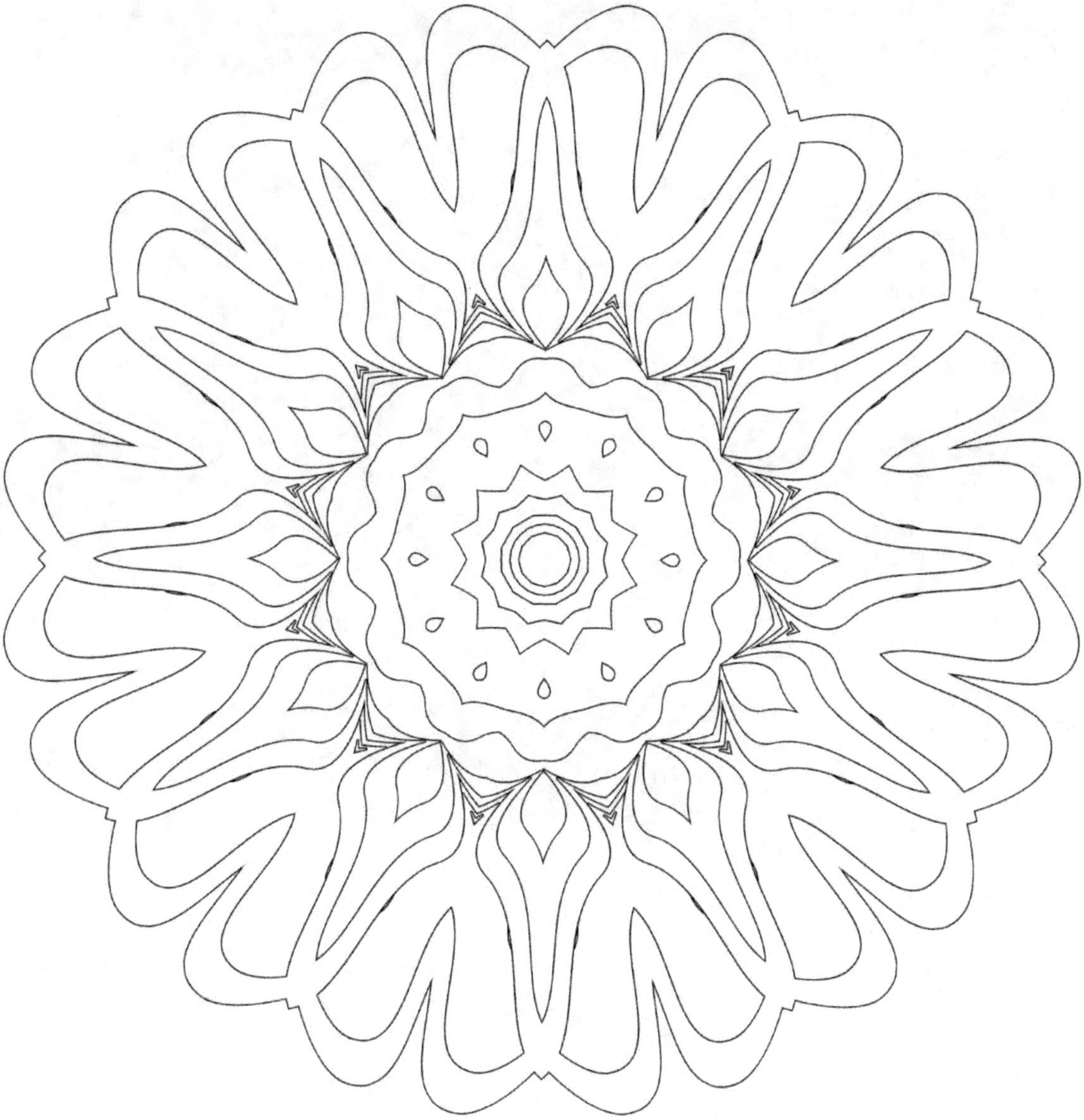

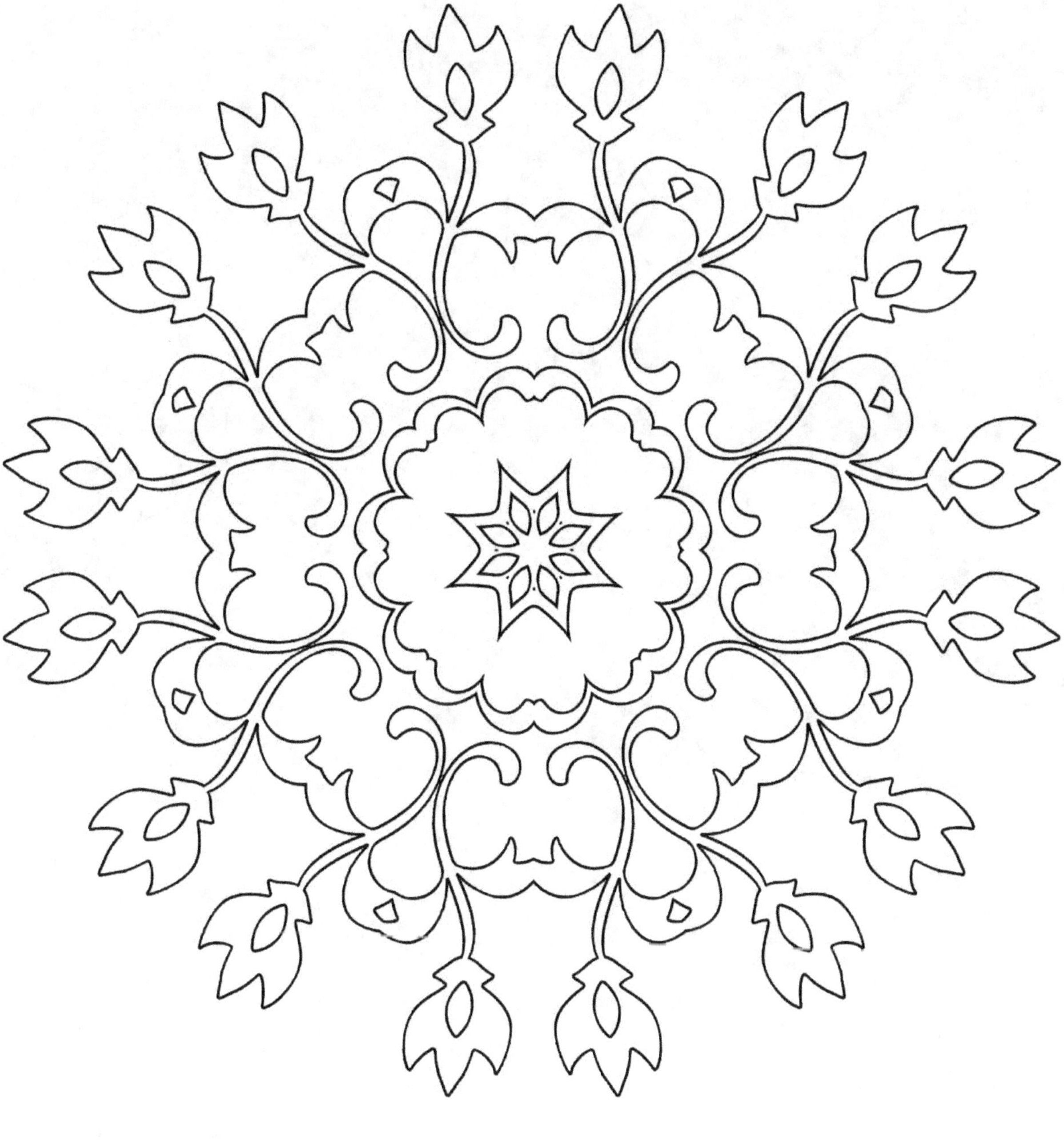

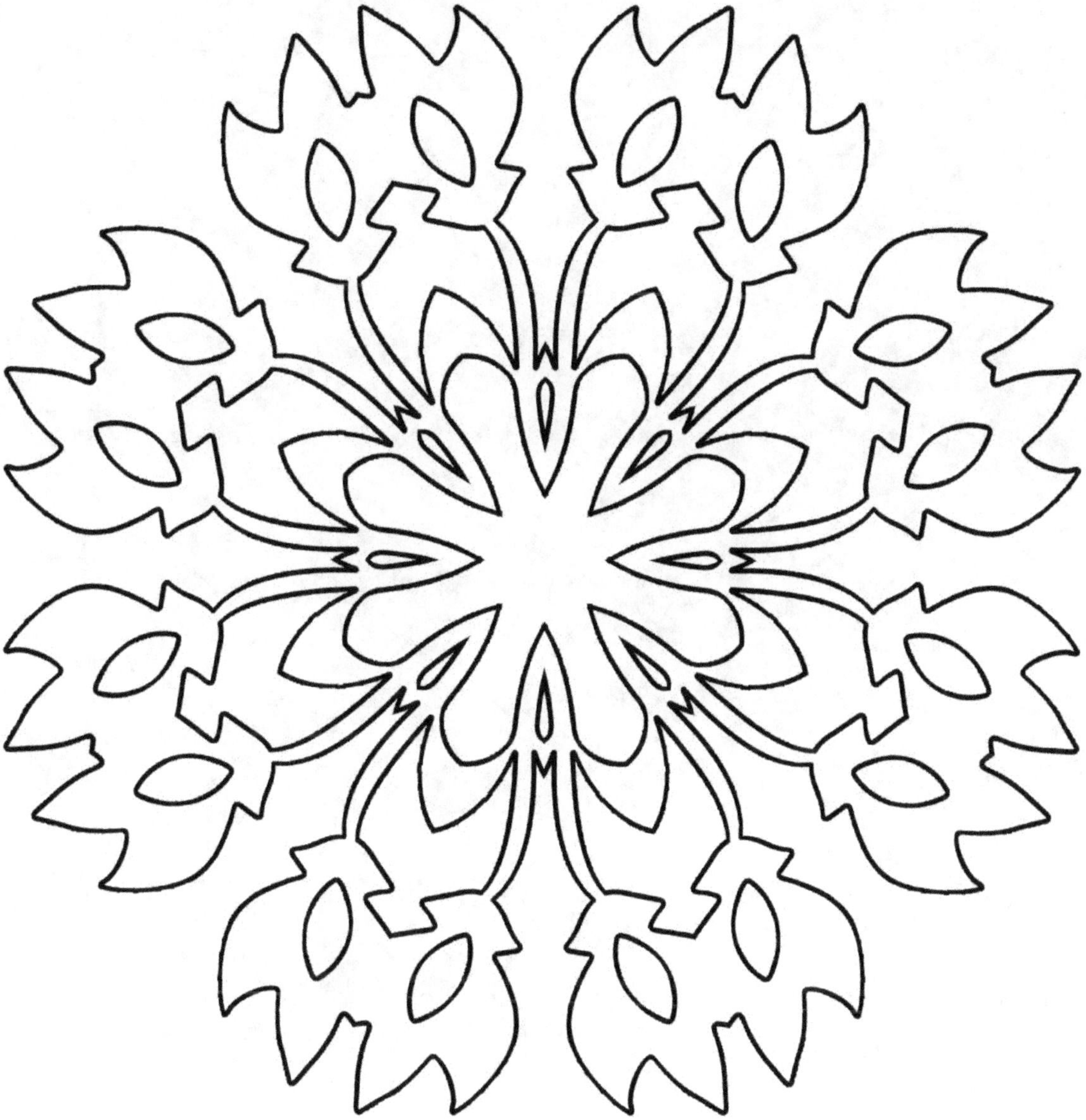

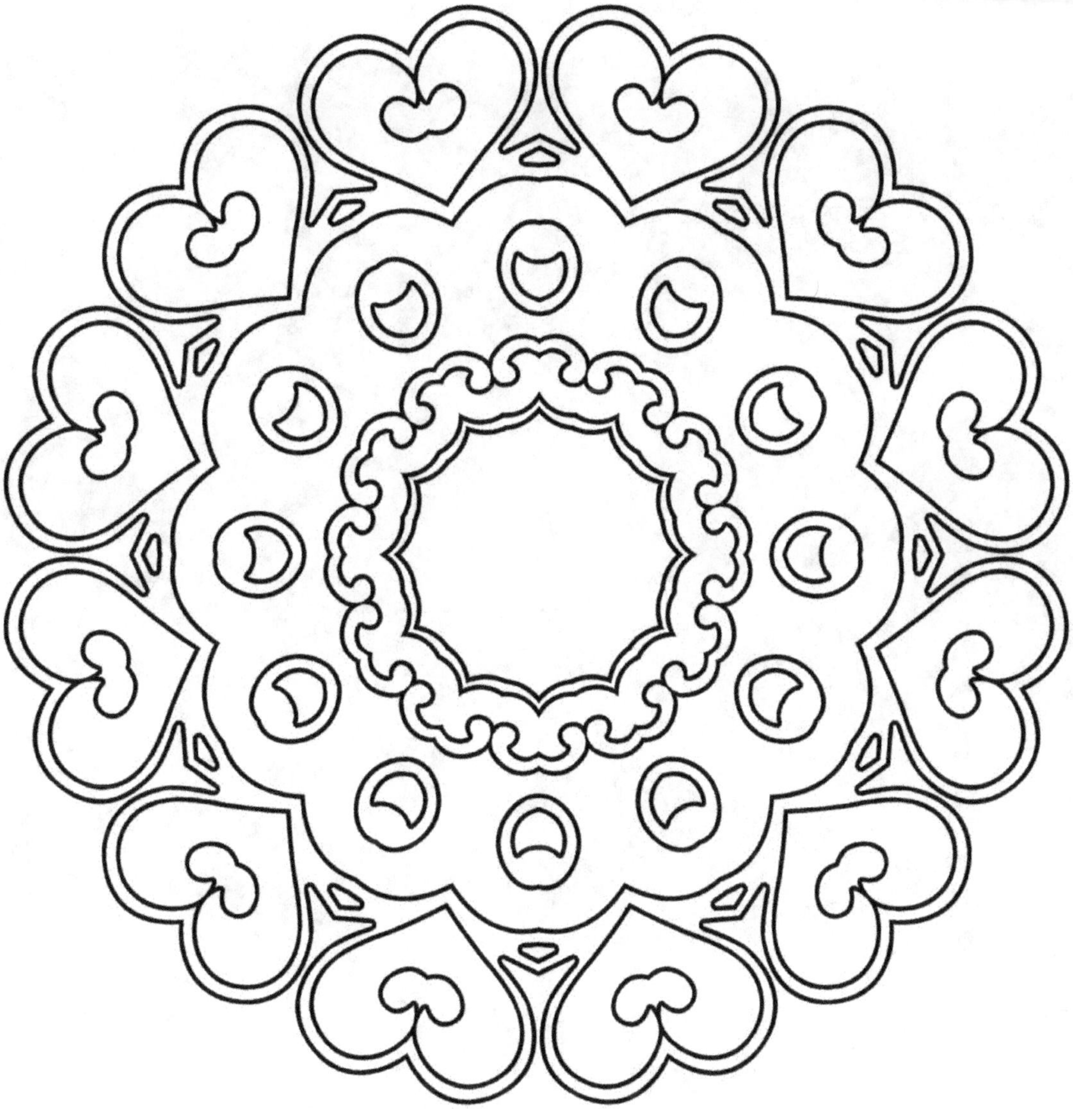

Thank you

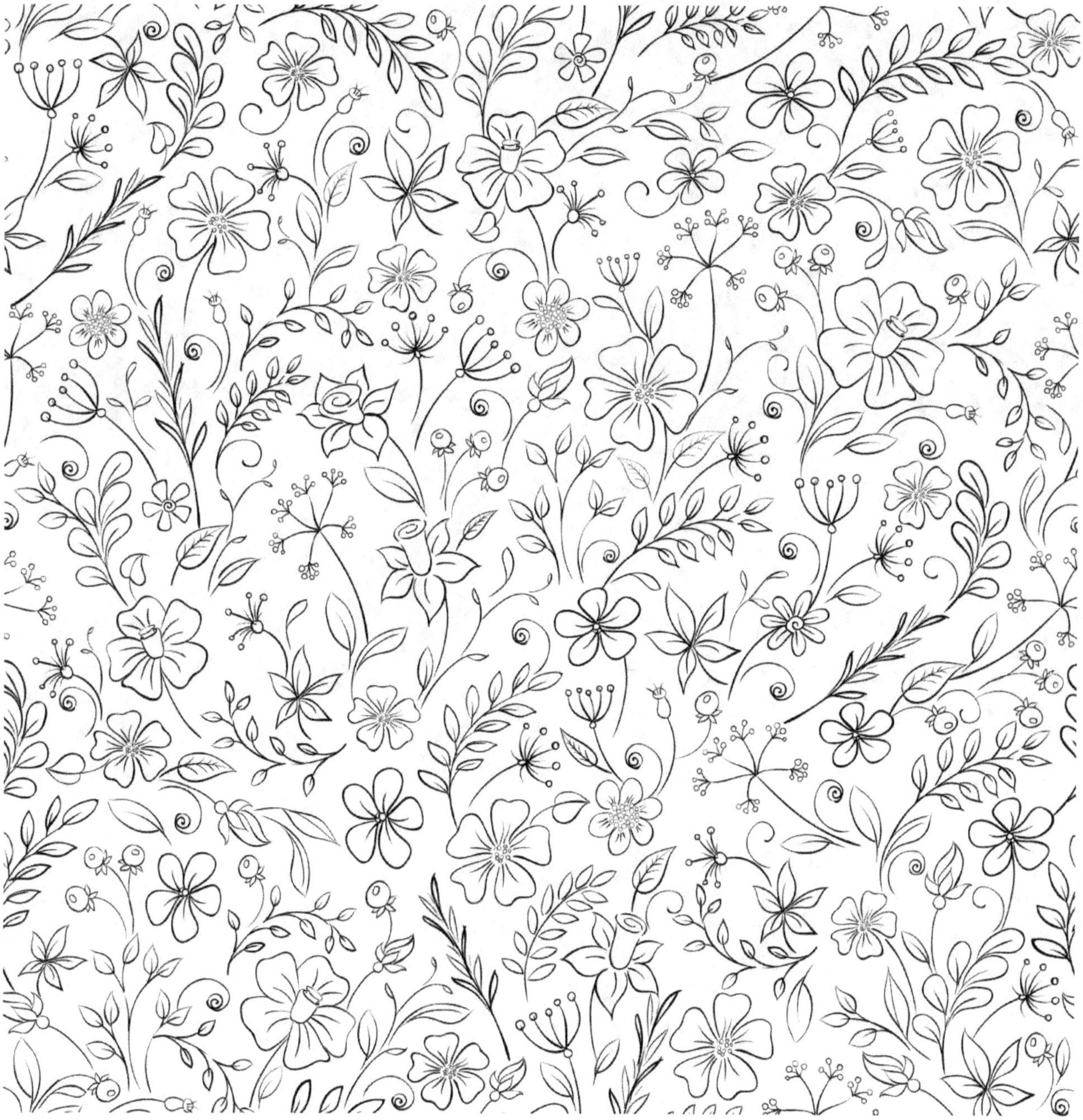

www.ingramcontent.com/pod-product-compliance
Lightning Source LLC
Chambersburg PA
CBHW081125180526
45170CB00008B/3016
* 9 7 8 1 5 4 2 6 4 8 8 3 7 *